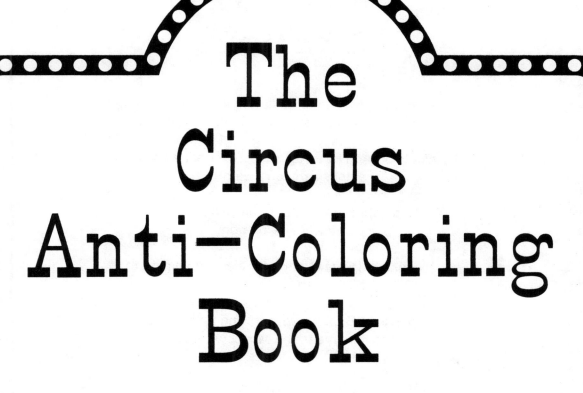

The Circus Anti-Coloring Book

Susan Striker

with
Jason Striker

Illustrations by Frank Magadan

An Owl Book
Henry Holt and Company
New York

In loving memory
of Uncle Eddie

Thanks to Greg Hamlin for believing in and supporting the
anti-boring, anti-stifling concept of learning

Thanks to Jo Ann Haun for taking over editing with skill,
enthusiasm, and warmth

Thanks to Chris Tomasino for always being there and
always being right

Thanks to Diana Crofton for elevating typing to
an art form

Thanks to Bob, for never giving up his efforts
to take me to the Moscow Circus

Henry Holt and Company, Inc.
Publishers since 1866
115 West 18th Street
New York, New York 10011

Henry Holt® is a registered
trademark of Henry Holt and Company, Inc.

Published in Canada by Fitzhenry & Whiteside Ltd.,
195 Allstate Parkway, Markham, Ontario L3R 4T8.

ISBN 0-8050-3412-9

Henry Holt books are available for
special promotions and
premiums. For details contact:
Director, Special Markets.

First Edition—1994

Printed in the United States of America
All first editions are printed on acid-free paper.∞

1 3 5 7 9 10 8 6 4 2

The Anti-Coloring Book is a registered trademark
of Susan Striker.

Introduction

The circus has a long tradition of being a family-oriented affair; not only because it is wonderful family entertainment, but because performing families are a circus tradition. Many performers grow up living with the circus, having watched their own parents train and work there. As early as they can, the children of performers help with chores and begin to learn circus arts and skills.

There once was a time when most children grew up in the same fashion: learning by helping their families. By doing farm chores, watching and caring for younger brothers and sisters, preparing meals, or helping out with the family business, children began to prepare for the responsibilities of adult life. The realities of today, however, make it more likely that both Mom and Dad are off doing work that remains a mystery to the kids, the babies are in day care, and meals are more likely to be "picked up" than prepared. Now we demand that more and more learning take place in school rather than at home. Families come together on weekends and vacations, exhausted from work and looking for relaxation and entertainment. Just when the need for meaningful family entertainment is greatest, we find X-rated language and violence on TV, in the movies, and in multimedia games and toys. With no more time or inclination to worship together, families play killer video games and cheer on heroes who kill and maim their adversaries in ways never before imagined. It is a difficult and stressful time in which to grow up. We need to do more together as families and do things that promote the ideals we believe in.

I, for one, would rather see an acrobat master gravity than one more police car chase, would rather enjoy a clown's humorous or poignant commentary than hear one more raunchy joke from a dysfunctional-family sitcom, and I'll never tire of the majesty of that elephant parade in the grand finale. There is no way we can pass along everything our children will need to know, but we *can* share with them our personal vision and a sound philosophy of life. That, after all, is the only legacy that counts. While I can't protect my child completely from the gory entertainments of the twentieth century, I trust that having been able to share my ideals with him will help make him a better man. I was grateful and reassured that the circus came to town year after year, providing hours of great family entertainment.

When my son was an infant I held him in my left arm and drew pictures for *The Third Anti-Coloring Book* with my right. As a toddler he fingerpainted with his apple sauce and chocolate pudding and inspired me to write two books about creativity in the very young: *Young at Art* and *Please Touch*. When he was three and angry that I was working on a book instead of taking him to the playground, he stamped his foot at me and demanded to know why I had never written a book for him about his favorite superheroes. *The Superpowers Anti-Coloring Book* was in bookstores a year later and was given as the favor at his next birthday party. Over the years Jason posed for several book covers and activity pages, and as he grew older, he regularly contributed project ideas to Anti-Coloring Books and advised me on how to keep my teaching ideas "cool." It was for Jason that we went on a yearly excursion to the circus where one year, while sitting under the big top, it suddenly dawned on me that the circus would be a great theme for many inspiring art activities. I pulled out my pad and began to write. The next year Jason brought his pad along to the circus and our latest family adventure had begun! Jason is fourteen years old as this book goes to press. He brought to the project a fresh vision and enthusiasm that continues to inspire me. I hope he learned a little something from me as well. Even if he never writes another book, he had to benefit from sharing this experience with me. You don't need to have a career as glamorous as a circus performer to want to pass along to your children the essence of who you are.

Creating *The Circus Anti-Coloring Book* was a rewarding family experience for us. When life gets difficult, instead of running away from your family to join the circus, as many have dreamed of doing, run away *with* your family . . . and mine! Artists have been inspired to paint the circus since it began. Join them and Jason and me as we create our own circus. Together we can experience thrills, danger, excitement, glamour, superhuman skills, lots of laughs, and a close-up view of some of the greatest creatures of nature.

—Susan Striker

Glossary of Terms

aerial: in the air

buffoon: clown, prankster

commemorate: honor

enthrall: enchant, fascinate, captivate

equestrian: a rider or circus performer on horseback

extravaganza: an elaborate, spectacular theatrical production

flank: to be on the side of something

hippodrome: an arena for a circus

levity: lightness or gaiety, frivolity

ornately: overly adorned, heavily ornamented

pachyderm: large, thick-skinned, hoofed animals including the elephant, rhinoceros, and hippopotamus

perilous: dangerous

precariously: uncertainly, insecurely, dangerously

wizardry: magic, sorcery

Hooray! This joyous and colorful banner announces that the circus is coming to town.

Acrobats performing death-defying tricks while riding bareback are said to have created the world's very first circus in 1768.

These clowns are famous for the ridiculous hats they wear.

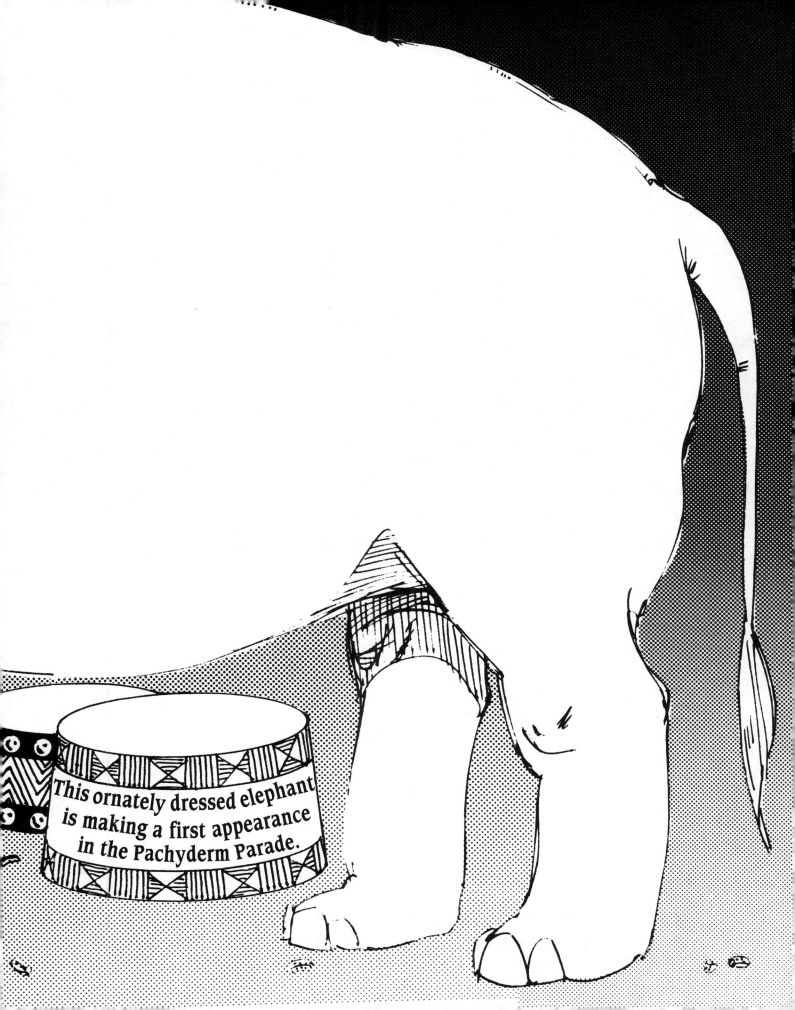

This ornately dressed elephant is making a first appearance in the Pachyderm Parade.

The fearless wild animal trainer is leading the animals through their daring and dangerous new act, being seen for the first time by the public in today's extravaganza.

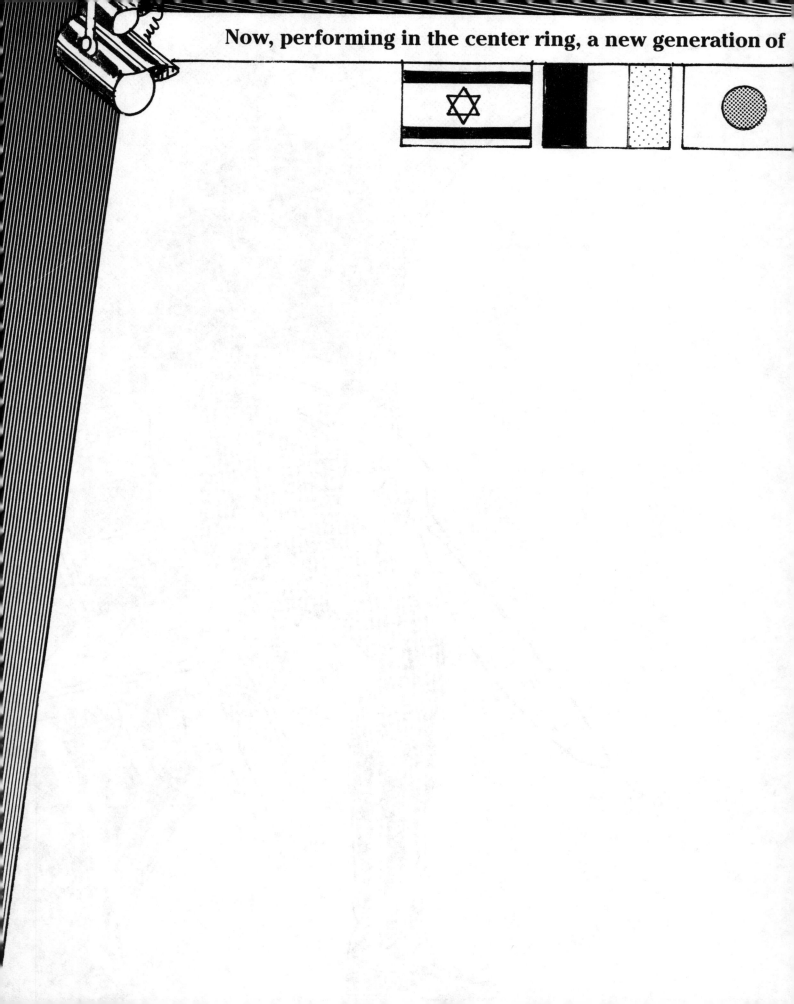

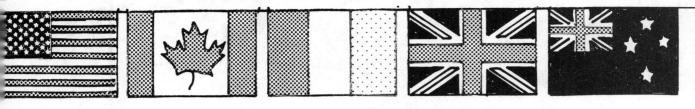

Circus

Picture yourself joining the circus and displaying a remarkable talent.

Auditions Today!

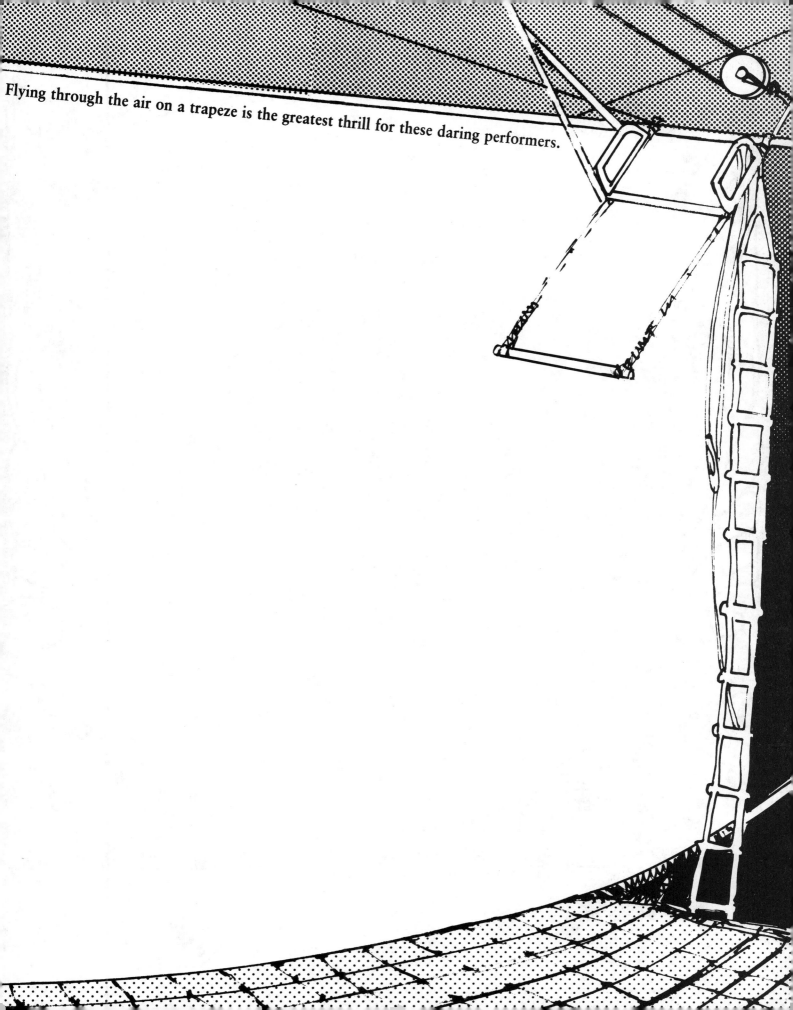

Flying through the air on a trapeze is the greatest thrill for these daring performers.

INTRODUCING:
The Strongest Person on Earth

INTRODUCING:
The Most Tattooed Person Ever Seen

In defiance of danger, these bicycle buffoons amaze the crowd with their daredevil act.

These clowns
One sad, one happy
all skillfully create

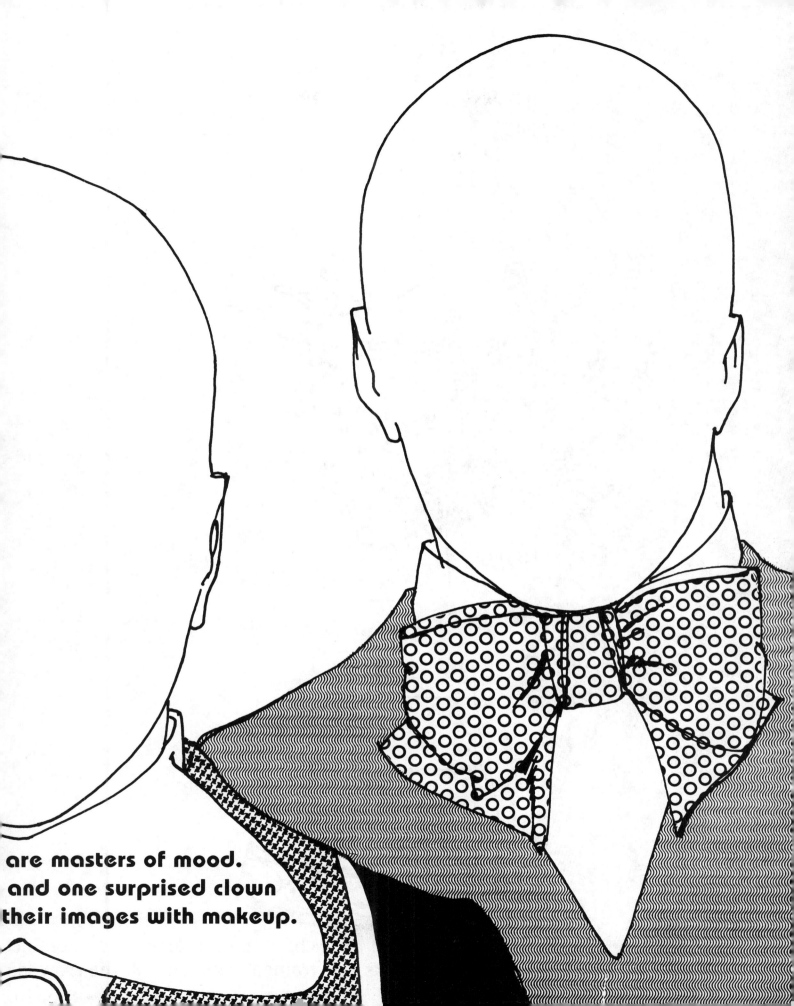

are masters of mood.
and one surprised clown
their images with makeup.

With their charming costumes and adorable tricks, the trained dogs enthrall the crowds.

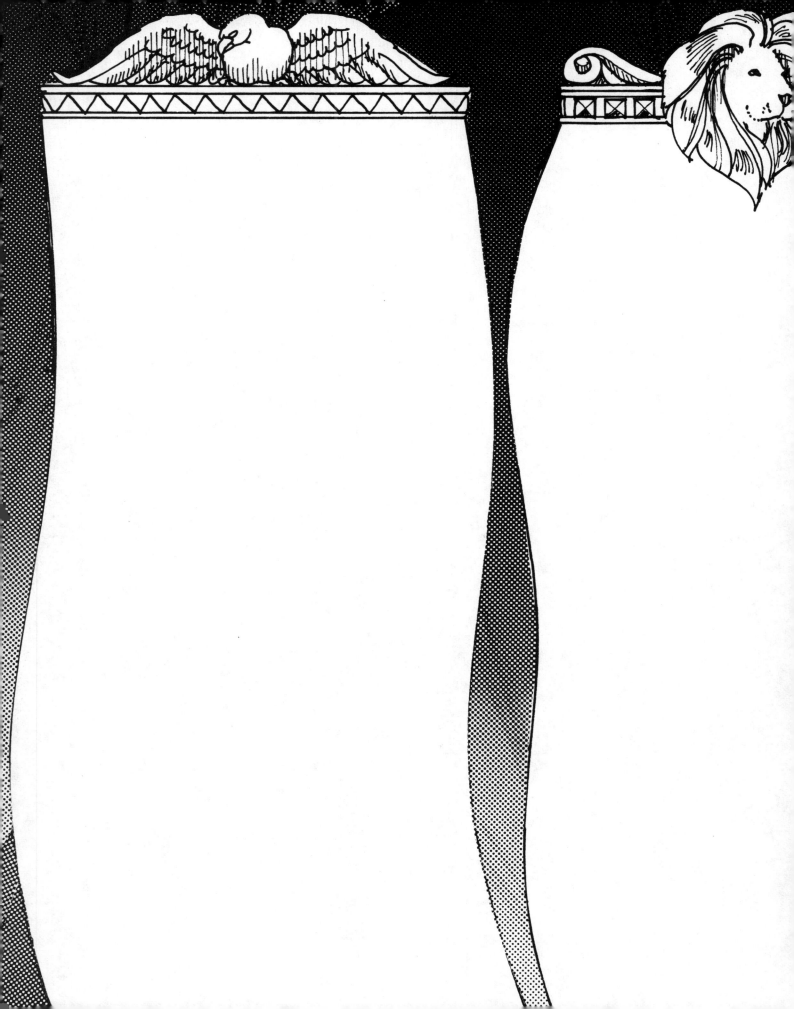

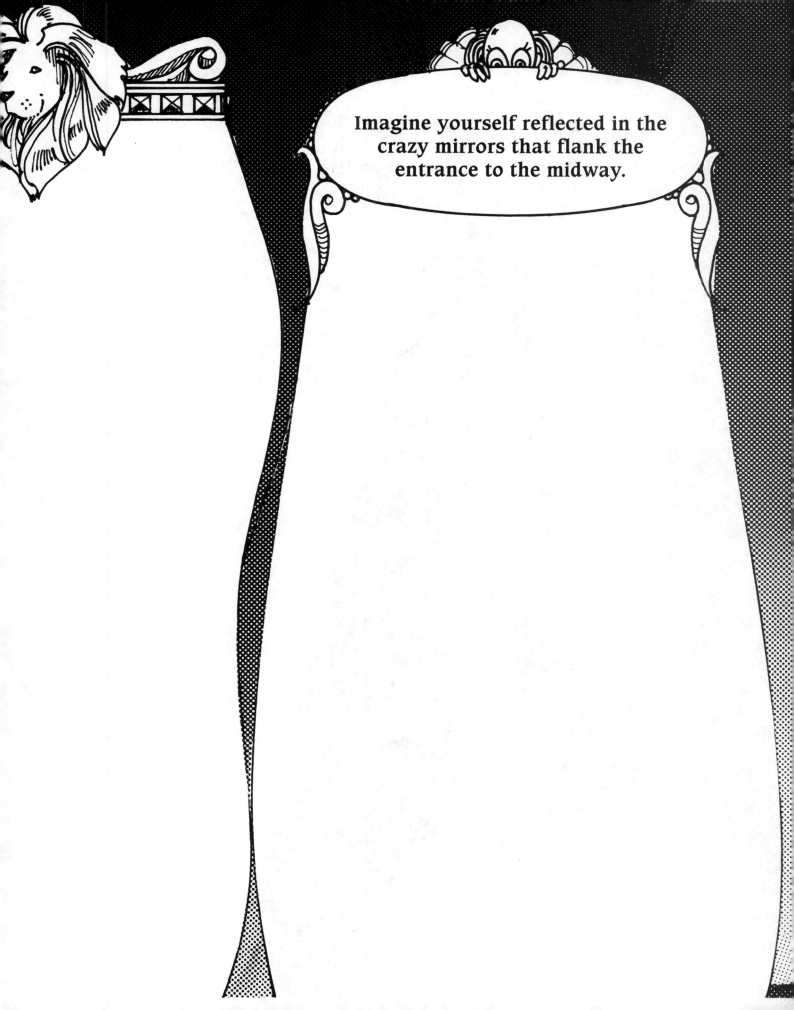

Imagine yourself reflected in the crazy mirrors that flank the entrance to the midway.

In the center ring is an impressive equestrian
demonstration, featuring different breeds
of horses and talented riders in fanciful costume!

At intermission, all of the children in the audience put on a sparkling light show.

Ladies and gentlemen and children of all ages, the circus is proud to

announce the most breathtaking display of aerial wizardry ever seen!

*A Wild West rodeo is this year's
action-packed theme attraction.*

The clowns are tipping their hats with lighthearted levity to the circus's most beautiful and glamorous dancers in their glittery costumes.

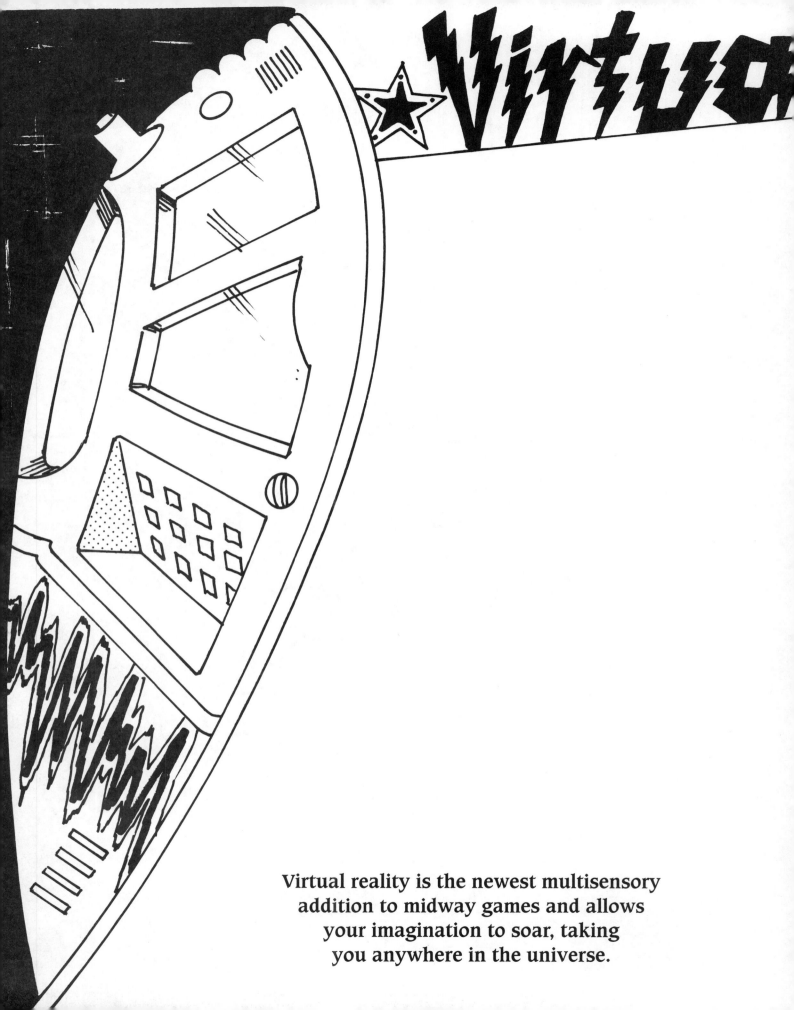

Virtual reality is the newest multisensory
addition to midway games and allows
your imagination to soar, taking
you anywhere in the universe.

REALITY

Ringling Brothers and Barnum and Bailey Circus
8607 Westwood Center Drive
Vienna, VA 22182

CIRCUS CIRCUS HOTEL
2880 LAS VEGAS BLVD. S.
LAS VEGAS, NEVADA 89109

Clyde Beatty-Cole Bros. Circus
P.O. Box 127
Deland, FL 32721

**Design some postage stamps to commemorate
all that is best about the circus.**

Bentley Bros. Circus
1926 NE 147 Terrance
Miami, FL 33181

CIRCUS GATTI
P.O. Box 3967
TUSTIN, CA 92681

Big Apple Circus
35 West 35 Street
New York, N.Y. 10117

It seems impossible to figure out
how so many clowns can fit into this tiny car.

At intermission, almost everyone
finds the souvenirs irresistible.

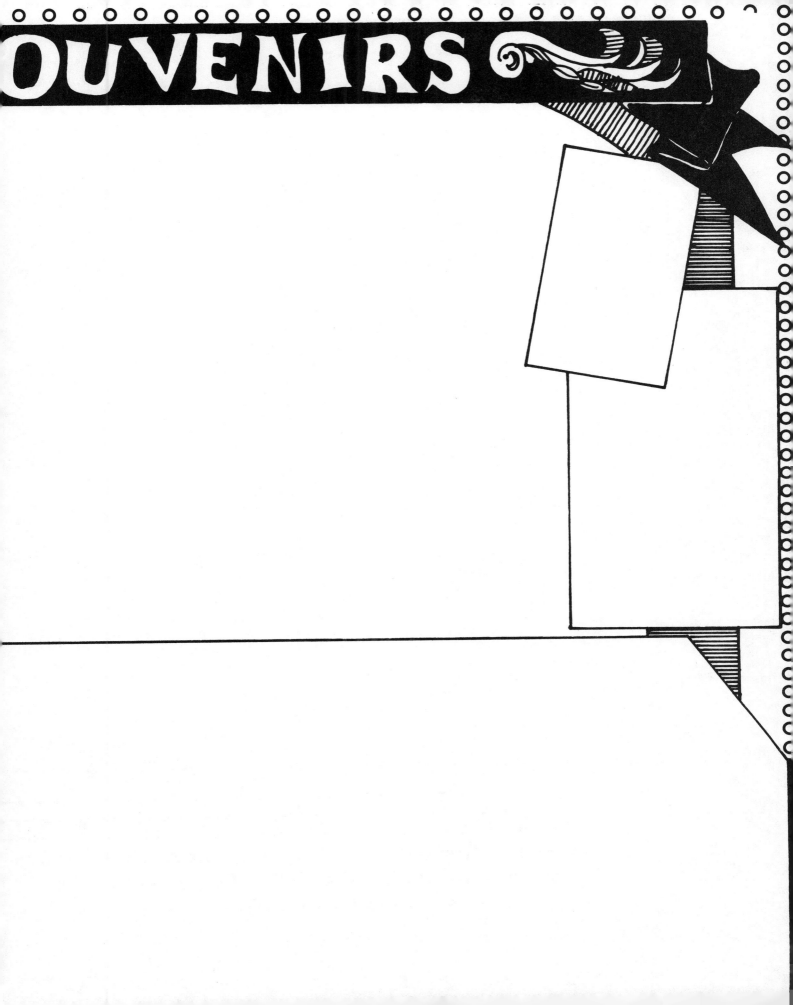

OUVENIRS

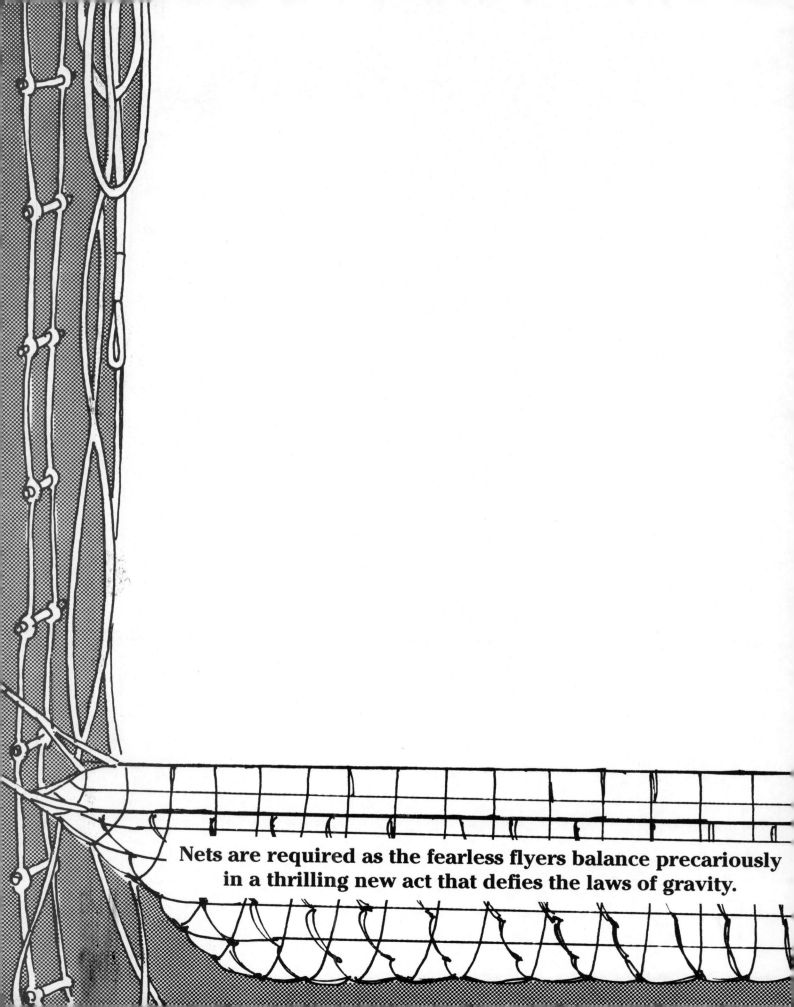

Nets are required as the fearless flyers balance precariously
in a thrilling new act that defies the laws of gravity.

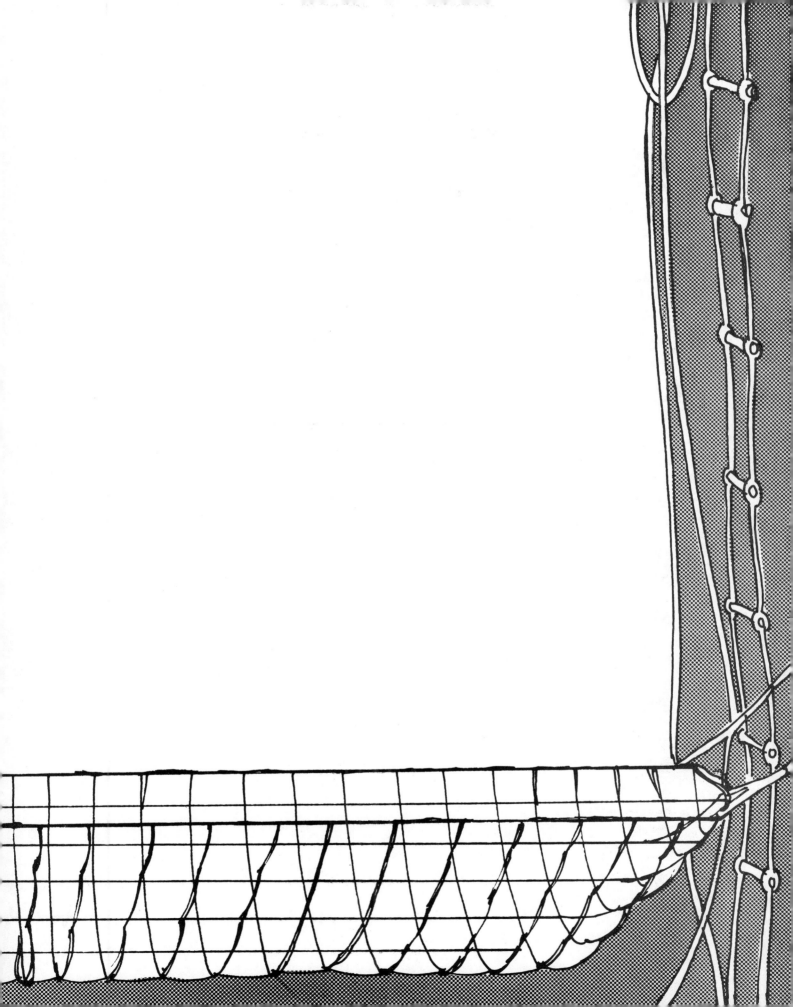

You won tickets to see the
showcase of new circus stars.

This clown is ready, willing, and able to make you up for your first circus appearance.

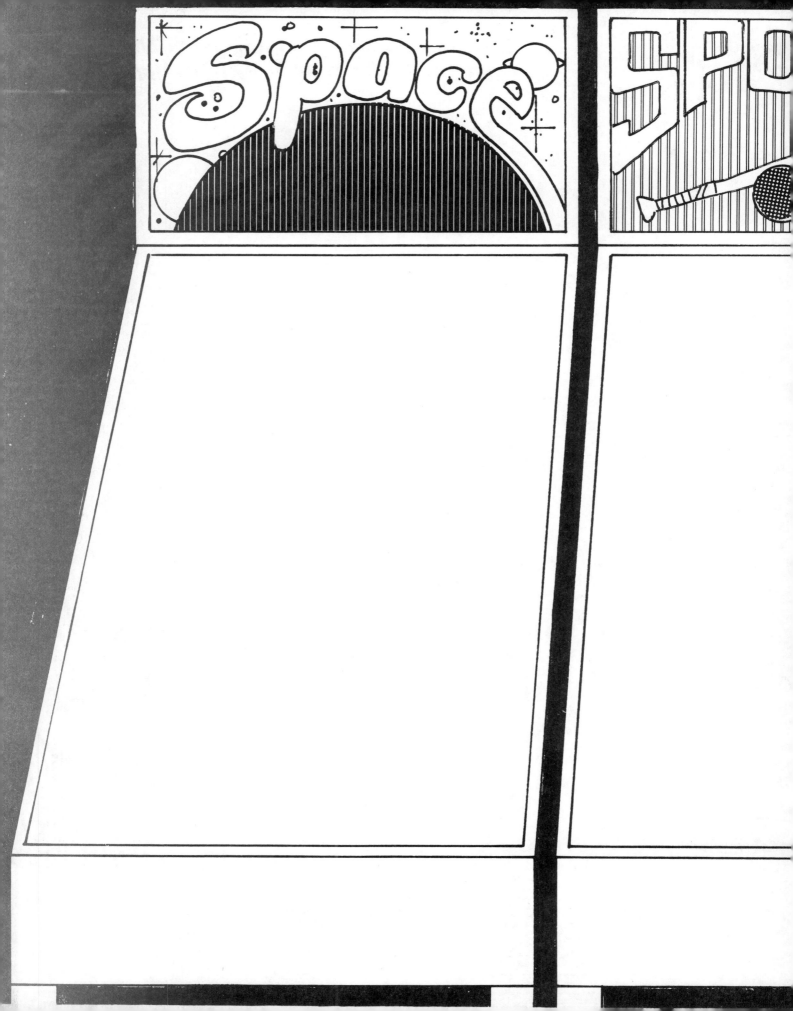

Beauty Queen

There are intriguing and challenging
video games in the modern midway
to capture just about anyone's fancy.

Everyone is spellbound watching the daring tightrope act as the acrobats risk life and limb in a perilous performance high above the hippodrome.